Iona Community

eNemy OF APaThy

by

JOHN BELL & GRAHAM MAULE

with

The Wild Goose Worship Group

songs

VOLUME 2
Songs of the Passion and
Resurrection of Jesus, and
the Coming of the Holy Spirit.

First Published 1988

Revised 1990

Dedicated

to

RON, IAN and KATHY

with

love and gratitude

for

all their new beginnings.

®™

The Wild Goose is a Celtic symbol of the Holy Spirit.
It serves as the Trademark of Wild Goose Publications.

© Copyright 1988 The Iona Community   ISBN 0 947988 27 0

Wild Goose Publications

The Publishing Division of the Iona Community
Pearce Institute, 840 Govan Road, Glasgow G51 3UT
Tel: 041 – 445 4561

CONTENTS

E – JESUS, ON THE ROYAL ROAD

F – JESUS, RESURRECTED

G – THE HOLY SPIRIT, COMING TO STAY

H – CHANTS AND RESPONSES

AN
INTRODUCTION
TO
ENEMY OF APATHY
WILD GOOSE SONGS
VOLUME TWO

(The Wild Goose is one of the Celtic symbols for the Holy Spirit)

We said enough in the introduction to Volume One about the background to the songs and the way in which they came about. We also included an elementary guide on teaching songs which holds good for all the material in this book.

Volume Two starts, as Volume One ended, with Jesus on the move, making his incessant demand that people should be converted not to an idea of God, but to the experience of a journey. It was "Come and follow me" he said, not "Rest and remember."

Thus in the first section, JESUS – ON THE ROYAL ROAD, we sing of and with the Lord who in every action re-interpreted what kingship meant. It demanded that he should be obedient, appear as a servant and take the consequences for refusing to conquer by unbridled power. The world was to be redeemed by suffering love, not subjugated by divine tyranny. So, on the royal road, we find Jesus weeping and saddened not for himself, but for the people and city which refused to recognise the signs of the times.

In JESUS – RESURRECTED, the second section, we sing of the triumph of love and of the real Jesus who met real disciples on the third and subsequent days.

Because there is always the temptation to enshrine the resurrection in past history, the songs point both to the need for resurrection in present day life and to the presence of the risen Christ who, even yet, meets us in the guise of the stranger before we recognise him as the Lord.

The concluding section of songs, GOD THE SPIRIT COMES TO STAY, is incomplete. It deals primarily with Pentecost and the promises of Christ to his followers. But there are many more aspects of the Spirit's activity in the Church, in the ministries of healing and prayer, in the sacraments and ceremonies of life. These make the basis of the third volume of *Wild Goose Songs*, entitled *Love From Below*.

Many of the songs in this collection were either written for or inspired by the annual retreat at Iona Abbey and Youth Centre entitled *Experiencing Easter*. We were privileged to share in its inception and have, in successive years, marvelled at what happens when ordinary people from all over Britain come together to look closely at what happened to Jesus during Holy Week, to reflect on that in terms of their own experience, and to celebrate the agony and the joy in worship.

It was during these events that we saw clearly how, through minimising the spoken (or preached) word and maximising music, colour, movement and symbols, the Passion and Resurrection came alive even for the dourest cynic and most word-bound presbyterian. And it was during these events that the Peter, Thomas, Judas and Mary Magdalene in ourselves were identified as we met, lost and were found again by Jesus in a new way.

We shared the planning and running of these events with Ian and Kathy Galloway, Wardens of Iona Abbey, with the constant encouragement of Ron Ferguson, Leader of the Iona Community. At *Experiencing Easter*, as elsewhere, they, more than any, have shown for us and for the Wild Goose Worship Group that kind of unnerving trust which both witnesses to and evinces faith in the Christ who loves and dies and lives again. To them we gratefully dedicate this book.

The songs are all biblically based and find their roots in the accounts of the last weeks of Christ's earthly ministry and the earliest days of the young church. That is not to suggest that they are designed for exclusive use during Lent, Easter and Pentecost. Every week has its own losses, betrayals and triumphs to celebrate, and, as our spiritual ancestors insisted, every Sunday should be a re-presentation of Christ's resurrection.

John L. Bell
Graham A. Maule
February 1988

Please note: In this revised edition there are guitar chords given with some songs. These do **not** always correspond to harmony settings.

JESUS, ON THE ROYAL ROAD

PREPARE THE WAY OF THE LORD

Tune: HOLY JOHN (JLB)

moderato

When the faith of God's peop-le was low,
PRE———PARE THE

Dm   Gm7

WAY OF THE LORD!   no —one knew where the Spir—it would   blow.

Am7   D   Dm

PRE———PARE THE WAY OF THE LORD! PRE (desc.) PARE THE

Gm7   Am7   D   Gm   Am7

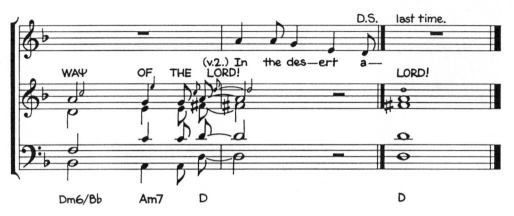

1.   *Cantor* : When the faith of God's people was low,
      All   : PREPARE THE WAY OF THE LORD!
      Cantor : No one knew where the Spirit would blow.
      All   : PREPARE THE WAY OF THE LORD!
              PREPARE THE WAY OF THE LORD!

2.   *Cantor* : In the desert, alone in his cell, ...
              God let John know the news he should tell. . . . .

3.   *Cantor* : Like a tinker he looked, as he cried, ...
              Calling his nation to Jordan's near side. . . . .

4.   *Cantor* : There he announced the Messiah would come, ...
              Saviour of all but a let-down for some. . . . .

5.   *Cantor* : "Turn in your tracks and prepare a new way! . . . .
              He might come tomorrow, he could come today." . . . .

6.   *Cantor* : Holy John was familiar and strange, ...
              A voice in the desert, demanding all change. . . . .

As it was John the Baptist who prepared the way for Jesus, it is fitting that we should remember him as we begin to follow the road Christ took to the cross.

Whether this song is accompanied or not, the response sung by everyone should not be too obtrusive.

FINDING GOD

Tune: ST. PATRICK (Irish Trad.)

confidently

Where can we find the God who made and wants us for his ve——ry own? How can we know the God by whom all that is yet to be is known? When shall we meet the God whose name each age has called on, cursed and blessed, the God by whom both cos——mic power and new born ba——by are ad—dressed?

1. Where can we find the God who made
   And wants us for his very own?
   How can we know the God by whom
   All that is yet to be is known?
   When shall we meet the God whose name
   Each age has called on, cursed and blessed,
   The God by whom both cosmic power
   And new born baby are addressed?

2. God's found where human life is prized,
   And human worth affirmed and warmed;
   Where hated hearts become forgiven
   And untouched lives become transformed;
   In lantern face of wisdom's age,
   In wide-eyed children's fresh rapport,
   In those with whom he bids us share
   The things that heaven and earth are for.

3. God's found where silence is not feared —
   The silence which we seldom seek
   In case our consciences rebel
   Or God, in confidence, should speak;
   The silence when our souls assess
   Unfathomed sense conveyed by sound,
   And that magnificence of love
   Upon which heaven and earth are ground.

4. God's found where he was set aside —
   The last upset where faith went blind,
   The fond, fake image still embraced
   In the school playground of our mind;
   Or in the test we set the Lord
   To prove his interest, show his powers
   To change the world to suit our will
   As if both heaven and earth were ours.

5. God's found in following Jesus Christ,
   Who summons all to set aside
   The mess and masks of daily life
   Behind which things we often hide.
   The finding comes through following close,
   Inspired by trust, surprised by grace;
   Both, contradicting common sense,
   Make all of heaven and earth God's place.

A harmonised version of the tune will be found in most hymnbooks, often in association with the words, "I bind unto myself today."

To sing this well, let a soloist take verse 1, a choir or group verse 2, women verse 3, men verse 4, all verse 5.

COME, TAKE MY HAND

Tune: THE BRAES O' KILLIECRANKIE (Scottish Trad.)

brightly

Come take my hand and be my friend: your
health and hope I'll glad—ly mend; your worth,though hid—den,
I'll re—veal, your brok—en—ness I'll touch and heal.
AND IF YOU WILL GO WHERE I WILL GO, ON
PATH—WAYS SMOOTH AND TROU-BLE-SOME,AND IF YOU WILL LOVE AS
I WILL LOVE, YOU'LL SEE ON EARTH THE KING-DOM COME.

Words © 1988 The Iona Community

1. Come take my hand and be my friend:
    Your health and hope I'll gladly mend;
    Your worth, though hidden, I'll reveal,
    Your brokenness I'll touch and heal.

Chorus : AND IF YOU WILL GO WHERE I WILL GO,
            ON PATHWAYS SMOOTH AND TROUBLESOME,
            AND IF YOU WILL LOVE AS I WILL LOVE,
            YOU'LL SEE ON EARTH THE KINGDOM COME.

2. O leave the things that let you down:
    The lust for wealth or cheap renown,
    The memory of what you've been,
    The worst you've ever thought or seen.

3. Prepare to welcome those who like
    Your hand to shake or face to strike.
    The love I share, which saves the lost,
    Is never cheap but comes at cost.

4. I am the bread, I am the wine,
    I lay my lifeblood on the line.
    If you're with me, avoid pretence:
    Stay on the ground and not the fence.

As with several other words set to folk tunes, this is best sung using a
solo voice for the verses, and everyone joining in the chorus.

JAIRUS' DAUGHTER

Tune: SHE WALKS THROUGH THE FAIR (Irish Trad.)

at a differing pace

The home holds a still—ness, the walls ech-o fear; the dar—ling, the daugh-ter, to death now draws near. So, send for the teach-er with heal—ing for skill; bring him to the bed—side where the young lass lies ill.

1.   The home holds a stillness, the walls echo fear;
     The darling, the daughter, to death now draws near.
     So, send for the teacher with healing for skill;
     Bring him to the bedside where the young lass lies ill.

2.   Their journey scarce started, the word travelled fast
     That the angel of death through the household had passed.
     Yet forward together walked father and guest.
     "Your faith has convinced me to grant your request."

3.   The women were wailing, well versed in their chore,
     Half-mourning the child whom their dirges were for –
     A girl of good nature, cut off in her prime.
     No need now for healing. No need to waste time.

4.   *"Look not to their grieving; look not to your grief.*
     Your daughter is sleeping through death to relief.
     The end of this matter defies your sad stare.
     My touch on her hand will answer your prayer."

5.   The mourners find laughter to douse their fake tears;
     Rejecting God's mercy, they covet their fears.
     Their cheeks are not stained with salt water, but scorn.
     Of genuine compassion their grief was not born.

6.   *"Move out of my pathway! Move out of my sight!*
     Blind fools, you interpret the wrong for the right.
     Your words and your wailing, your sighs and your leers
     Are proof that true wisdom has not come with years."

7.   The mother and father and friends of God's will
     Accompany Christ where the daughter lies still.
     There, through word and gesture, she comes to her feet,
     And, for her, the Saviour asks something to eat.

8.   *"Tell no one what happened, but rejoice in God's power.*
     What's done must be secret, at least for this hour.
     My words are not spells to cure all who are ill:
     My word is the witness that health is God's will."

This is not a congregational song. It is best suited to the telling or miming of the story of Jairus' Daughter, as found in Mark chapter 5. Two or more voices can be used to sing the narrative – one being that of Jesus.

The verses should not be sung in strict tempo, but their speed and expression varied according to the mood of the words. The beautiful Irish melody is well suited to this purpose.

TEARS OF SORROW

Tune: TEARS OF SORROW (JLB)

gently

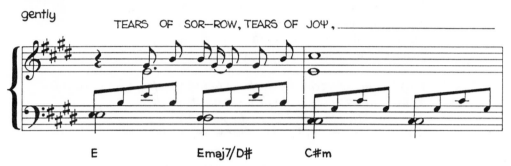

TEARS OF SOR—ROW, TEARS OF JOY, _____

E   Emaj7/D#   C#m

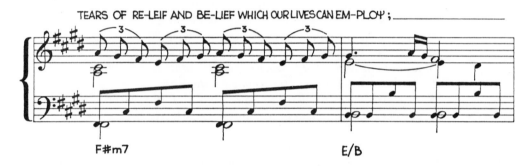

TEARS OF RE-LEIF AND BE-LIEF WHICH OUR LIVES CAN EM-PLOY; _____

F#m7   E/B

TEARS OF PLEAS-URE, TEARS OF PAIN, _____

E   Emaj7/D#   C#m

TEARS THRO' WHICH GOD CAN TOUCH OUR LOSS AND TURN IT IN—TO GAIN. last time
to coda.

A   G#m   F#m7   B

3 part Harmony. Look at Christ on his roy—al road, lett——ing pass-ion and

C#m   F#/C#   C#m7   F#/C#   Amaj7   F#m7

grief ex—plode : Je—sus weeps for a friend who's gone —

G#   C#m   F#/C#   C#m7   F#/C#

no ex—cep——tion, God's on—ly son.   D.C. except verse 4.

Amaj7   F#m7   Bsus4

Interlude after verse 4. (piano only)

Coda after last chorus.   Fine.
D.C.

Bsus4   E

Words and Music © 1988 The Iona Community

Chorus : TEARS OF SORROW, TEARS OF JOY,
TEARS OF RELIEF AND BELIEF WHICH OUR LIVES CAN EMPLOY;
TEARS OF PLEASURE, TEARS OF PAIN,
TEARS THROUGH WHICH GOD CAN TOUCH OUR LOSS
AND TURN IT INTO GAIN.

1. Look at Christ on his royal road,
Letting passion and grief explode:
Jesus weeps for a friend who's gone –
No exception, God's only son.

2. Sister, brother, parent, friend –
Those whose touch now has reached its end –
I can clutch or I can set free,
Free to wait till they welcome me.

3. From the womb, through the mother's groans,
Comes the child as she screams and moans:
Come life's close, we take on the pain
To be born into life again.

4. Death's a door we need not conceal;
Death, like life, is both raw and real.
Hide the truth and you live a lie,
Fight the tears and God's strength you deny.

This song is primarily about death and bereavement, but takes its starting point from Jesus' own ability to show grief openly on hearing of the death of Lazarus.

It is good if this song is sung at times other than when there is a bereavement, as part of accepting death and bereavement is the ability to talk about such issues when they are not on the immediate horizon.

If possible, three part women's voices should take the verses.

JERUSALEM, JERUSALEM

Tune: BROOD (JLB)

slowly & expressively

Je — ru — sa-lem, Jer— ru — sa-lem, you mur——der the

proph——ets and sil—ence those God sends you.

Words and Music © 1988 The Iona Community

1. Jerusalem, Jerusalem,
   You murder the prophets
   And silence those God sends you.

2. How many times
   I wanted to embrace you!
   But you would never let me.

3. Therefore your homes,
   Your city and your temple
   Will be, by God, forsaken.

4. Never again
   Will you know my presence
   Until you meet me, saying,

5. "Blessed is he
   Who comes in the name,
   In the name of the Lord."

Luke places these words of Jesus prior to the entry into Jerusalem,
Matthew places them after. Either way, they are appropriate for Holy
Week.

Note the slight variations in rhythm, especially in verses 1 & 4. Sing,
unaccompanied, slowly and expressively.

RIDE ON, RIDE ON

Tune: RIDE ON (JLB)

resolutely

Ride on,____ ride on,____ the

time____ is right: ____ the road ____ side crowds_ scream

with ____ de — light; ____ palm branch-es mark the pil-grim way where

beg-gars squat and child — ren play. _____ v.2. Ride (Fine.)

Words and Music © 1988 The Iona Community

1. Ride on, ride on, the time is right:
   The roadside crowds scream with delight;
   Palm branches mark the pilgrim way
   Where beggars squat and children play.

2. Ride on, ride on, your critics wait,
   Intrigue and rumour circulate;
   New lies abound in word and jest,
   And truth becomes a suspect guest.

3. Ride on, ride on, while well aware
   That those who shout and wave and stare
   Are mortals who, with common breath,
   Can crave for life and lust for death.

4. Ride on, ride on, though blind with tears,
   Though dumb to speak and deaf to jeers.
   Your path is clear, though few can tell
   Their garments pave the road to Hell.

5. Ride on, ride on, the room is let,
   The wine matured, the saw is whet;
   And dice your death-throes shall attend
   Though faith, not fate, dictates your end.

6. Ride on, ride on, God's love demands.
   Justice and peace lie in your hands.
   Evil and angel voices rhyme:
   This is the man and this the time.

This is a processional song. If not actually sung by people moving, a similar effect can be gained by starting with one voice and gradually increasing the number of people singing until the end. It finishes abruptly and dissonantly because, in many ways, the Palm Sunday procession was just the beginning.

An evident alternative tune is *Winchester New*, found in most hymn-books with the words "Ride on, Ride on in majesty."

I WAS GLAD

Tune: NEW 122nd (JLB)

steadily

I was glad when they said to me, _____ "Let us

go to the house of the Lord." _____ And

look, now we stand in that place, _____ in the

ci — ty be — lov — ed of God. _____

1. I was glád when they sáid to mé,
   "Let us gò to the hóuse of the Lórd."
   And lóok, now we stánd in that pláce,
   In the cíty belóved of Gód.

2. Jerúsalem próudly is búilt
   To gáther all péople togéther:
   She wélcomes the chíldren of Iśrael
   As they wórship their Máker in únity.

3. Hére they give thánks to the Lórd,
   Accórding to Gód's own desíre,
   In the cóurt of the kíngs of Iśrael
   By the thrónes of the hóusehold of Dávid.

4. Práy for the péace of Jerúsalem:
   "May they prósper whose lóve is for yóu.
   Péace be withín your wálls
   And prospérity bé in your pálaces."

5. For the sáke of my fámily and friends
   I will sáy, "May God's péace be with yóu."
   Out of lóve for the hóuse of the Lórd,
   I will práy for your wélfare foréver.

6. Glóry to Gód the Creátor,
   To the Són and the Hóly Ghóst
   As it wás in the beginning is nów
   And shàll be foréver, Amén.

This is a paraphrase of Psalm 122, one of the psalms used by pilgrims on or after their arrival in Jerusalem. It gains an added poignance if used in association with the activity of Jesus in the temple during Holy Week.

The doxology (verse six) is not obligatory. The psalm is much more authentic without, but occasion or custom might, in some places, require its inclusion.

For those unaccustomed to singing words which are pointed, the general rule is that those words with points above them fall on the first or third beat of the bar. Thus in verses 3, 4 and 6, the verse begins on the first beat of the first complete bar of music.

I WILL GIVE WHAT I HAVE

Tune: DE WILLE (JLB)

moderato

From a high, sec-ret shelf, I take what I hid my-self – per-fume,

pre-cious and rare, nev-er meant to spill or spare. This I'll care-ful-ly break, this I'll

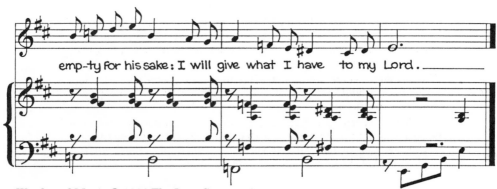

emp-ty for his sake: I will give what I have to my Lord._____

1. From a high, secret shelf, I take what I hid myself –
   Perfume, precious and rare, never meant to spill or spare.
   This I'll carefully break, this I'll empty for his sake:
   I will give what I have to my Lord.

2. Though the action is crude, it will show my gratitude
   For the truth that I've learnt from the one who's heaven-sent;
   For this life once a mess which his beauty can express,
   I will give what I have to my Lord.

3. With his critics around, common gossip will abound.
   They'll note all that they see to discredit him and me.
   Let them smirk, let them jeer, say what people want to hear;
   I will give what I have to my Lord.

4. It's because he'll receive, that the likes of me believe
   God has time for the poor. He has shown us heaven's door.
   Be it perfume and care, be it anger or despair,
   I will give what I have to my Lord.

It is the woman who visits Jesus in the house of Simon the Leper, (see Matthew chapter 26), who is represented in this solo song.

The tune is slightly reminiscent of the kind of French café song in which the words are half spoken and half sung.

THE PAWNBROKER

Tune: PAWNBROKER (JLB)

soulfully
V.1. only

Dreams to sell, dreams to sell: buy the brok-en prom-is-es the

world knows so well. Sad my theme, sad my theme,

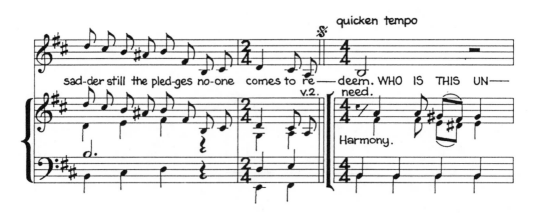

quicken tempo

sad-der still the pled-ges no-one comes to re——deem. WHO IS THIS UN——

v.2. need.

Harmony.

LIC—ENSED BROK-ER WHO AT—TEMPTS TO MOCK US LIKE A JOK —ER?

Food for all? Food for all? — Hun-ger and star-va-tion are still

shelved on my stall. Sense—less greed, sense—less greed

high—er ranks than just-ice, yet ful—fills no—one's —deem.

D.S. last time.

1. *Cantor* : Dreams to sell,   dreams to sell:
Buy the broken promises the world knows so well.
Sad my theme,   sad my theme,
Sadder still the pledges no one comes to redeem.
   All   : WHO IS THIS UNLICENSED BROKER
WHO ATTEMPTS TO MOCK US LIKE A JOKER?

2. *Cantor* : Food for all?   Food for all? —
Hunger and starvation are still shelved on my stall.
Senseless greed,   senseless greed
Higher ranks than justice, yet fulfils no one's need.
   All   : POINT NO FINGER AT OUR TREASURE!
CHARITY WE'VE SHOWN IN SOME SMALL MEASURE!

3. *Cantor* : People healed?   People healed?
Pompous prayers and piety have kept much concealed.
Still they groan,   still they groan:
Few will love and touch the lost whom God calls his own.
   All   : MUST WE TAKE THIS IMPOSITION?
PRAYER, NOT DEEDS, HAS LONG BEEN OUR TRADITION!

4. *Cantor* : Peace to last?   Peace to last?
Priceless new deterrents prove that pledge is surpassed.
War no more?   War no more?
What protects the rich is always paid by the poor.
   All   : CLEARLY YOU LACK ALL PERCEPTION!
TALK OF PEACE IS NOTHING BUT DECEPTION!

5. *Cantor* : Dreams to sell,   dreams to sell:
Buy the broken promises the world knows so well.
Sad my theme,   sad my theme,
Sadder still the pledges no one comes to redeem.

In this song Jesus is depicted as a pawnbroker, reminding people of the pledges that they have made but have not come back to redeem. The chorus confronts him, angrily, in the way that the scribes and pharisees did in the week prior to the crucifixion when, as Matthew chapter 23 indicates, his language was far from gentle.

HYMN OF THE PASSION

Tune: QUEM PASTORES (German Trad.)

moderato

Je—sus, don——key - carr——ied trea——sure, palm - waved prince, the peop——le's plea—sure pounds to heaven in man—gled mea—sure: loud ho—san—nas fill the sky.____

Words © 1988 The Iona Community

1. Jesus, donkey-carried treasure, palm-waved prince, the people's pleasure
   Pounds to heaven in mangled measure: loud hosannas fill the sky.

2. Jesus, temple trade upsetter, gilt-edged greed needs every debtor;
   Rescue faith from human fetter: turn the tables, let love fly.

3. Jesus, friend of saint and sinner, winner's loss and loser's winner,
   Bread of life and host of dinner, on your food we must rely.

4. Jesus, shame-faced Peter's brother, mocked by soldiers, mourned by mother,
   Pilate's crowd must choose another: "Free Barabbas!" is their cry.

5. Jesus, man of God neglected, Jesus, God in man rejected,
   Crucified and unprotected: "It is finished!" shout and die.

6. Lord, in mercy, pardon send us; Lord, from our worst selves defend us;
   By your broken body mend us, let our prayers be heard on high.

A harmonised version of the tune *Quem Pastores* will be found in most hymnbooks. Here it is used to enable us to think reflectively on some of the highlights of Holy Week. Slides or symbols may be used to accompany the words.

THE SONG OF THE SUPPER

Tune: AFTON WATER (Scottish Trad.)

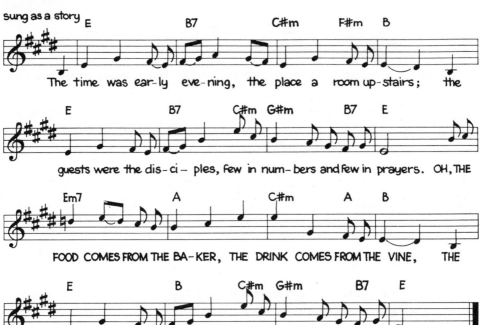

sung as a story

The time was ear-ly eve-ning, the place a room up-stairs; the guests were the dis-ci-ples, few in num-bers and few in prayers. OH, THE FOOD COMES FROM THE BA-KER, THE DRINK COMES FROM THE VINE, THE WORDS COME FROM THE SAV-IOUR, "I WILL MEET YOU IN BREAD AND WINE."

Words © 1988 The Iona Community

1. The time was early evening,
    The place a room upstairs;
    The guests were the disciples,
    Few in number and few in prayers.

Chorus : OH, THE FOOD COMES FROM THE BAKER,
            THE DRINK COMES FROM THE VINE,
            THE WORDS COME FROM THE SAVIOUR,
            "I WILL MEET YOU IN BREAD AND WINE."

2. The company of Jesus
    Had met to share a meal,
    But he, who made them welcome,
    Had much more to reveal.

3. *"The bread and body broken*
    The wine and blood outpoured,
    The cross and kitchen table
    Are one by my sign and word."

4. On both sides of the table,
    On both sides of the grave,
    The Lord joins those who love him
    To serve them and to save.

5. Lord Jesus, now among us,
    Confirm our faith's intent,
    As, with your words and actions,
    We unite in this sacrament.

On occasions, when the sacrament of Holy Communion is not being celebrated, verse 5 should be omitted. Wherever possible the words of verse 3 should be sung solo.

This is a particularly effective song for a house communion or, as happens at Iona Abbey on Maundy Thursday, when the sacrament is celebrated in the Refectory, the usual eating place.

LET YOUR RESTLESS HEARTS
BE STILL

Tune: THE LARK IN THE CLEAR AIR (Irish Trad.)

very gently

Let your rest-less hearts be still, let your trou—bled minds be rest—ed; trust in

KY——RI——E EL—EI————SON,

God to lift your care and, in car-ing, trust in me. In God's

KY——RI——E EL—EI————SON,

house you have a place— were it o—ther-wise, I would have told you—this I

KY——RI——E EL—EI————SON,

36

glad—ly go to pre—pare and make rea-dy for you all.

KY———RI——E EL——EI————SON.

Choir: KYRIE ELEISON, KYRIE ELEISON,
          KYRIE ELEISON, KYRIE ELEISON.

1.   *Solo* : Let your restless hearts be still,
              Let your troubled minds be rested;
              Trust in God to lift your care
              And, in caring, trust in me.
              In God's house you have a place –
              Were it otherwise, I would have told you –
              This I gladly go to prepare
              And make ready for you all.

2.   *Solo* : Where I am and where I'll be,
              Is where you shall live forever;
              And the way to where I go
              I have walked among you here.
              I'm the Way that never ends,
              I'm the Truth that never changes,
              I'm the Life that never dies
              But delights to love you all.

Choir: KYRIE ELEISON, KYRIE ELEISON,
          KYRIE ELEISON, KYRIE ELEISON.

These words are a paraphrase of part of Jesus' farewell discourse as recorded in John chapter 14.

A choir or group should sing the Kyrie (the words mean "Lord have mercy") before and after the solo verses. During the solo verses they hum their parts quietly.

O GIVE THANKS TO THE LORD

Tune: NEW 106th (JLB)

not too quickly

It is good to give thanks to the Lord, _____ to re-mem-ber all he has done.____Then God will re-mem-ber our prais — es, when he looks with love on his peo-ple.____

Harmony.

O GIVE THANKS TO THE LORD, _ FOR HIS LOVE EN-DURES FOR EV —— ER;

O GIVE THANKS TO THE LORD, _ FOR THE LORD A-LONE IS GOOD.____

1. It is good to give thanks to the Lord,
   To remember all he has done.
   Then God will remember our praises,
   When he looks with love on his people.

Response: O GIVE THANKS TO THE LORD,
FOR HIS LOVE ENDURES FOR EVER;
O GIVE THANKS TO THE LORD,
FOR THE LORD ALONE IS GOOD.

2. Our sin is the sin of our fathers,
   We have done wrong, we all have been evil.
   Like those who once lived in bondage,
   We paid no heed to all you had done.

3. Our fathers forsook your love:
   At the Red Sea, they questioned their God;
   They fell from their faith in the desert
   And put God to the test in the wilderness.

4. Time after time he would rescue them,
   Yet in malice they dared to defy him.
   Despite this he came to their aid
   When he heard their cries of distress.

5. Save us, O Lord, in your love.
   Bring us back from all that offends you.
   Look not alone at our sins,
   But remember your promise of mercy.

6. Blessed be the Lord God of Israel
   Both now and through all eternity.
   Let nations and people cry out
   And sing, Amen! Alleluia!

At the time of the Passover the Jews were, and still are, accustomed to recall the history of their experience of God as a nation. Psalm 106, of which the above is a paraphrase, brings these events to mind. It may therefore be fitting to use it as part of a Maundy Thursday communion service.

A cantor should sing all the verses solo, with everyone sharing the response.

O LORD MY GOD

Tune: O LORD MY GOD (JLB)

slowly and earnestly

O LORD MY GOD, O LORD MY GOD, WHY DO YOU SEEM SO

FAR FROM ME, O LORD MY GOD? _____ Fine.

FAR FROM ME, _____ O LORD MY GOD, MY GOD?

FAR FROM ME, O LORD, _____ O LORD MY GOD?

Night and morn—ing I make my prayer: _____ peace for

this place and help for there; _____ wait—ing and wonder—ing,

40

wait–ing and wonder–ing, does God care?___ Does God care?___

Words and Music © 1988 The Iona Community

Response: O LORD MY GOD, O LORD MY GOD,
WHY DO YOU SEEM SO FAR FROM ME,
O LORD MY GOD?

1. Night and morning I make my prayer:
Peace for this place and help for there;
Waiting and wondering,
Waiting and wondering,
Does God care?   Does God care?

2. Pain and suffering unbound and blind
Plague the progress of humankind,
Always demanding,
Always demanding,
Does God mind?   Does God mind?

3. Why, oh why do the wicked thrive,
Poor folk perish, the rich survive;
Begging the question,
Begging the question,
Is God alive?   Is God alive?

4. Turn again as you hear my plea;
Tend the torment in all I see:
Loving and healing,
Loving and healing,
Set me free.   Set me free.

This is a protest song or a complaint . . . in the way that around a third of the Psalms are not about telling God how good life is, but how lousy it is. This kind of stark honesty before God is seen *par excellence* on the cross when Jesus asks if he has been forsaken.

Sing this song, with a small group singing the verses, during Holy Week or at other times when it is appropriate to bring to God sorrow and upset as well as joy.

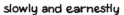

THE SERVANT

Tune: AE FOND KISS (Scottish Trad.)

slowly and earnestly

Who would ev——er have be—lieved it?

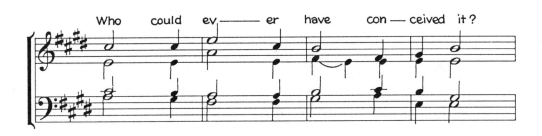

Who could ev——er have con—ceived it?

Who dared trace God's hand be—hind it

when a ser——vant came a—mong us?

1. Who would ever have believed it?
   Who could ever have conceived it?
   Who dared trace God's hand behind it
   When a servant came among us?

2. Like a sapling in dry soil,
   He was rooted in our presence;
   Lacking beauty, grace and splendour,
   No one felt attracted to him.

3. We despised him, we disowned him,
   Though he clearly hurt and suffered:
   We, believing he was worthless,
   Never turned our eyes towards him.

4. Yet it was the pain and torment
   We deserved which he accepted,
   While we reckoned his afflictions
   Must have come by heaven's instruction.

5. Though our sins let him be wounded,
   Though our cruelty left him beaten,
   Yet, through how and why he suffered,
   God revealed our hope of healing.

6. We, like sheep despite our wisdom,
   All had wandered from God's purpose;
   And our due in pain and anger
   God let fall on one among us.

7. Who would ever have believed it?
   Who could ever have conceived it?
   Who dared trace God's hand behind it
   When a servant came among us?

Isaiah, chapter 53, contains the passage which identified God's 'suffering servant'. These words, here paraphrased, are evocative both of how Christ, at the Last Supper, took the servant's place and of how, at his death, there was little about him which seemed godly.

CONTEMPORARY REPROACHES

Tune: REPROACHES (JLB)

slowly and sadly

I walked through the lone-ly streets,   and I sat with the face-less ones,

Dm   Dm7/C   Dm6/B   Gm7/Bb

and made friends with for-gott-en folk; _____ but   you nev-er saw me. _____

Am7/G   Bbmaj7/F   Gm6/E   Am7/E

quicken pace slightly

O LORD,   O WHAT HAVE WE DONE,___FOR WE NEV—ER FIND YOU A-MONG US?___

Dm   Gm7   Dm   Gm7   Am7   D

1. *Cantor* :   I walked through the lonely streets,
              And I sat with the faceless ones,
              And made friends with forgotten folk;
              But you never saw me.
    Response: O LORD, O WHAT HAVE WE DONE,
                   FOR WE NEVER FIND YOU AMONG US?

2. *Cantor* :   I stood close to your window pane,
              And I knocked on your tight shut door;
              But so full and busy is life,
              Who am I to disturb you?

3. *Cantor* :   I gave you a hammer and nails
              And wood from a living tree;
              And, just for the carpenter's son,
              What a present you made for me.

4. *Cantor* :   To those whose eyes were blind,
              I gave light so that they could see;
              But what can I do for you
              Whose look is seldom for me?

The idea of 'reproaches' comes from an ancient church liturgy for Good Friday in which the cantor, taking Jesus' part, reminds the congregation of the good that God has done and the evil shown in return.

When this setting is used the response should, in the first verses, be loud and angry, as if Christ should have been more evident in the world. Towards the end the response becomes quieter and more penitent.

The cantor should follow the natural rhythm of speech rather than keep a strict tempo for each verse. Extra notes will therefore be added *ad lib*.

LORD JESUS CHRIST,
SHALL I STAND STILL?

Tune: THE LEA RIG (Scottish Trad.)

should — ers fling the wrong I breed and con—tem—plate?

1. Lord Jesus Christ, shall I stand still
    And stare at you hung on the tree;
    Or shall I move to where you move
    And die and live again for me?
    Shall I to sin and failure cling,
    Consorting with the guilt I hate;
    Or on your shoulders shall I fling
    The wrong I breed and contemplate?

2. Shall I your story read and tell
    To note your mark on history;
    Or shall I make your story mine
    And live by faith and mystery?
    Shall I embrace the love you show
    And covet this sweet, holy thing:
    Or of that love shall my heart speak,
    My hands relate, my being sing?

3. Shall I retreat from where you fall
    And seek a safer path through life;
    Or shall I meet you in the world
    Where peace is scarce, injustice rife?
    Lord Jesus Christ, the God who lives
    To love and die and rise again,
    Make me the who, and you the why,
    Your way the how, and now the when.

If it would take longer than is available to teach this lovely Scottish tune, an immediate alternative is to use *Rockingham*, the tune most often associated with the words, "When I survey the wonderous cross."

WHEN THE SON OF GOD WAS DYING

Tune: GOLGOTHA (JLB)

steadily

When the Son of God was dy—ing long a——go,———

some played dice and some knelt cry—ing, lost and low.———

Cy—nics sneered and wagged their tongues, mock—ers mim—icked fune—ral songs:

this, while God's own son was dy—ing, long a—go.———

Words and Music © 1988 The Iona Community

1. When the Son of God was dying, long ago,
   Some played dice and some knelt crying, lost and low.
   Cynics sneered and wagged their tongues,
   Mockers mimicked funeral songs:
   This, while God's own Son was dying, long ago.

2. Crowds which once had cried, "Hosanna!", lost their voice:
   Hell had grinned to hear Barabbas was their choice;
   Judas hung himself for blame;
   Peter hung his head in shame,
   While the crowds which cried, "Hosanna!", lost their voice.

3. Horror, hurt and pain found home in Mary's breast
   Watching torture's toll and hearing soldiers jest:
   Where was God to hear her cry?
   Why should her own Jesus die?
   Grief and agony found home in Mary's breast.

4. Humankind repeats Golgotha every day:
   God gets gagged while friends and followers turn away.
   Profit threatens peace on earth,
   Greed to hunger gives new birth
   As the world repeats Golgotha every day.

5. Jesus, lay your body in this sad earth's grave;
   Only one who suffers can presume to save.
   End hypocrisy and lies,
   Through our apathy arise,
   Bring us the salvation which our spirits crave.

A song for Good Friday or any day on which we want to relate the death of Jesus, not just to Jerusalem, but to the need for salvation in the contemporary world and in ourselves.

AN EMPEROR OF FOOLS

Tune: GARGOYLE (JLB)

slowly and sadly
No-where state—ly, ser—ene or pret—ty,_____ but a

dump near a roy—al ci—ty____ hosts the crude cir-cus ring in

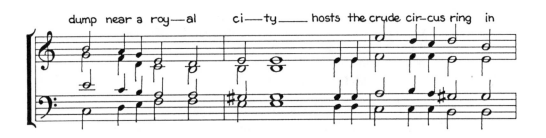

which a thorn-crowned king fa-ces Hell yet pro-claims his pi—ty._____

Words and Music © 1988 The Iona Community

1. Nowhere stately, serene or pretty,
   But a dump near a royal city
   Hosts the crude circus ring in which a thorn-crowned king
   Faces Hell yet proclaims his pity.

2. Like an emperor of fools he's treated —
   Speared and spat on, chastised and cheated;
   Searing pain, faltering breath are heralds of his death
   As his subjects deem him defeated.

3. Mary's silent and Peter's crying;
   Others shrink from his gaze, implying
   That, beneath all, they know the faith they failed to show
   Sealed the fate of the one who's dying.

4. See the monarch the world has wilted!
   See the saviour whom sin has silted!
   See the gargoyle of grace, grotesquely hung in space,
   Heaven's heir whom earth's justice jilted!

5. Take him down, you who stand and sorrow;
   Lay him low in the grave you borrow.
   Is his last rest a tomb . . . . or an enthroning room?
   Only God will reveal tomorrow.

As with all songs in this book, a healthy imagination in using them will be more helpful than a trained voice. This song will have little impact if everyone sings every verse. The congregation or group could be divided in two, taking alternate verses and let the last verse be sung solo or by a quartet, ending with a question rather than a conclusion.

TRAVELLING THE ROAD
TO FREEDOM

Tune: TRAVELLING (JLB)

steadily

Trav-elling the road to free — dom, who wants to trav — el the

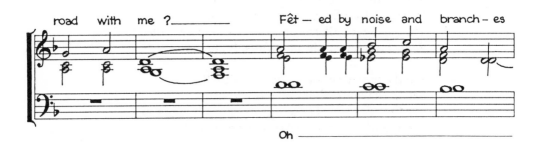

road with me ? _____ Fêt — ed by noise and branch — es

Oh _____

____ and ban-ners hang — ing from ev — ery tree; _____

(Oh) _____

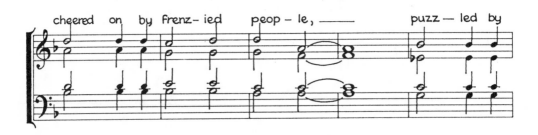

cheered on by frenz-ied peop-le, _____ puzz — led by

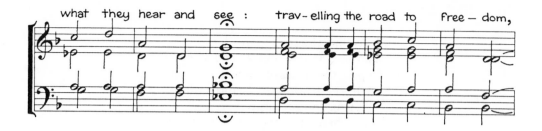

what they hear and see : trav-elling the road to free — dom,

___ who wants to trav — el the road with me ?___

1. Travelling the road to freedom,
   Who wants to travel the road with me?
   Fêted by noise and branches
   And banners hanging from every tree;
   Cheered on by frenzied people,
   Puzzled by what they hear and see:
   Travelling the road to freedom,
   Who wants to travel the road with me?

2. Travelling the road to freedom,
   Who wants to travel the road with me?
   Partnered by staunch supporters
   Who, come the dark, will turn and flee;
   Nourished by faith and patience,
   Neither of which is plain to see:
   Travelling the road to freedom,
   Who wants to travel the road with me?

3. Travelling the road to freedom,
   Who wants to travel the road with me?
   Tipping the scales of justice,
   Setting both minds and captives free;
   Suffering and yet forgiving,
   Even when my friends most disagree:
   Travelling the road to freedom,
   Who wants to travel the road with me?

4. Travelling the road to freedom,
   I am the Way, I'll take you there.
   Choose to come on the journey,
   Or choose to criticise and stare.
   Earth's mesmerising evil
   Only a traveller can repair.
   Travelling the road to freedom,
   I am the Way, I'll take you there.

If singing this song in harmony, the lower alto line can be taken by a solo tenor voice. The nature of the singing should be reserved and reflective rather than triumphant.

JESUS, RESURRECTED

WE NEED YOU, GOD

Tune: OFFENCE (JLB)

mysteriously

We fear you, God : you dare to come of—

—fend—ing from the vir—gin womb. Through this and through the

suck—ling breast, our sense of de—cen——cy you test till

world————ly life is weaned and blessed.

Words and Music © 1988 The Iona Community

1. We fear you, God:
    You dare to come
    Offending from the virgin womb.
    Through this and through the suckling breast,
    Our sense of decency you test
    Till worldly life is weaned and blessed.

2. We fear you, God:
    You dare enjoy
    The clothes and accents we employ.
    Through these and through the folk you meet,
    Eternity on earth you greet
    And shock pretentious faith's elite.

3. We fear you, God:
    You dare arrive
    Powerless and poor where tyrants thrive.
    Through this and through the naked cross,
    Security is charged with loss
    As love on hatred you emboss.

4. We need you, God,
    For you come near
    To where we are and what we fear.
    Our raw humanity you wear,
    Our limits to the tomb you bear
    Till these, redeemed by love, you share.

The chorale-like tune is best sung in four part harmony, with a sense
of apprehension, on the evening prior to Easter Day.

SING, MY SOUL

Tune: MYSIE (JLB)

gently

Sing, my soul, when hope is sleep — ing, sing when

faith gives way to fears; sing to melt the ice of

sad — ness, mak-ing way for joy through tears. —

Words and Music © 1988 The Iona Community

1. Sing, my soul, when hope is sleeping,
   Sing when faith gives way to fears;
   Sing to melt the ice of sadness,
   Making way for joy through tears.

2. Sing, my soul, when sickness lingers,
   Sing to dull the sharpest pain;
   Sing to set the spirit leaping:
   Healing needs a glad refrain.

3. Sing, my soul, of Him who shaped me,
   Let me wander far away,
   Ran with open arms to greet me,
   Brought me home again to stay.

4. Sing, my soul, when light seems darkest,
   Sing when night refuses rest,
   Sing though death should mock the future:
   What's to come by God is blessed.

This, essentially solo song, is a paraphrase of a letter from an elderly saintly woman whose testimony is that, even in her lowest days, when she speaks to God he listens, and then she sings to rejoice both her heart and his. It is well suited to the Saturday of Holy Week or to other occasions when loss or weakness are evident.

LORD OF THE MORNING

Tune: LORD OF THE MORNING (JLB)

Words and Music © 1988 The Iona Community

1. I tread on the grass where the dew lies deep
    While the air is clear and the world's asleep;
    I tramp on the verge of a dream that's gone –
    How I miss the Lord of the Morning!

    Morning!
    How can daylight dawn
    Now I miss the Lord of the Morning?

2. I trod through the streets on the resting day,
    Not a soul in sight, not a child at play;
    I tramped on the ash of a fire once bright –
    How I miss the Lord of the Morning!

    Morning!
    Let it still be night,
    For I miss the Lord of the Morning!

3.   I trod all the way from the town to the hill
      And I found my way, but I lost my will;
      I tramped up the stairs to a room turned strange –
      How I miss the Lord of the Morning!

           Morning!
           Nothing can derange
           How I miss the Lord of the Morning!

4.   I trod out the hours on a wine-stained floor
      Till the darkness warned of the day in store;
      I tramped to a garden, engulfed in dread –
      How I miss the Lord of the Morning!

           Morning!
           Life and love are dead
           And I miss the Lord of the Morning.

(PAUSE FOLLOWED BY CHANGE OF SINGER FOR LAST VERSE)

5.   I tread on the grass where the dew lies deep
      While the air is clear and the world's asleep;
      I tramp on the verge of an endless dawn –
      For I am the Lord of the Morning,

           Morning!
           Darkness now has gone
           And I am the Lord of the Morning!

The song should, until verse 4, be sung as the expression of the thoughts in the mind of Mary Magdalene as she comes to the tomb. These are therefore best sung by a female voice with, after the pause, a male voice taking the part of Jesus.

It is best sung in the darkness at midnight on the evening before Easter. The two singers need not be seen, but can be situated at the rear or either side of the sanctuary.

THE ROBBER

Tune: DOUBLECROSS (JLB)

majestically

Lest friends or mob_____ should storm or rob,_____ a

sen——try guards the grave,_____ till slaugh-tered

love and an-gels shove the bould——er, and, three days

(descant)

old——————er, the slain re——turns to save.

1. Lest friends or mob
   Should storm or rob,
   A sentry guards the grave,
   Till slaughtered love
   And angels shove the boulder,
   And, three days older,
   The slain returns to save.

2. The tomb is bare
   As women stare
   At where a corpse was laid.
   Then, through their fright,
   Sound matches sight: "He's risen!
     The Lord is risen
     Exactly as he said!"

3. Where mourners walk,
   Where strangers talk,
   Where weakness withers men,
   With great surprise
   He meets their eyes. He'll never,
   He'll never ever
   Be laid to rest again.

4. Death now has died:
   Christ has defied
   Its fear, its force, its sting.
   He robbed the grave!
   So sing brave alleluias,
   Sing alleluias
   To greet our risen king.

This song should be sung both majestically and joyfully and is best
accompanied by organ.

TORN IN TWO

Tune: SUSSEX CAROL (English Trad.)

Where sight and in — sight lose their way, we seg – re – gate fa-mil – iar ground from where we think you ought to stay and peace and par – a-dise a – bound: in Christ you tore this bar – rier down ____ – the Word made flesh let heaven be known. ____

Words © 1988 The Iona Community

1. Where sight and insight lose their way,
   We segregate familiar ground
   From where we think you ought to stay
   And peace and paradise abound:
   In Christ you tore this barrier down —
   The Word made flesh let heaven be known.

2. When Holy Grace took human form
   And called earth's outcast folk his friends,
   When Heaven's Original revealed
   The path required to make amends.
   We felt compelled to fret and fuss.
   You know — for you were here with us.

3. In warm embrace for withered arms,
   In dining out with tarnished guests,
   In breaking umpteen petty rules,
   In controversial, quiet requests,
   Barriers dividing heaven from earth
   Were bulldozed to reveal our worth.

4. Still, we are reticent to see
   That all of life is yours to save,
   That peace and poverty and power
   Adorn your birthplace and your grave,
   That, rising, you redeemed the fraud
   Of virtue trying to shelter God.

5. Ah, Holy Jesus, come again
   Wherever we would keep you out.
   Destroy our sanctimonious shrouds
   To demonstrate, to all who doubt,
   The temple's veil is torn in two
   And all of life is sacred now.

Don't let the tune, traditionally used at Christmas, put you off. It most appropriately carries the force of these words. For those unsure of the allusion in the last verse, Matthew chapter 27, verse 51, provides the answer.

CHRIST HAS RISEN

Tune: TRANSFORMATION (JLB)

gently

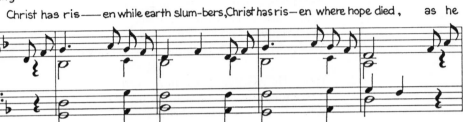

Christ has ris——en while earth slum-bers, Christ has ris—en where hope died, as he

Gm Am7 Bb Gm Am7 Dm

said and as he prom—ised, as we doubt——ed and de-nied. Let the

Gm Gm7 C Gm Gm7 C

moon em-brace the bless-ing; let the sun sus—tain the cheer; let the

Gm/Bb F/A Eb/G Gm7 C

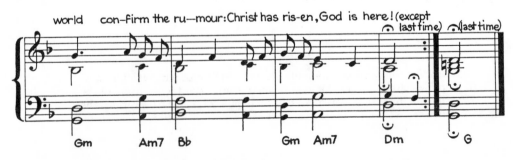

world con-firm the ru—mour: Christ has ris-en, God is here! (except last time) (last time)

Gm Am7 Bb Gm Am7 Dm G

1. Christ has risen while earth slumbers,
   Christ has risen where hope died,
   As he said and as he promised,
   As we doubted and denied.
   Let the moon embrace the blessing;
   Let the sun sustain the cheer;
   Let the world confirm the rumour:
   Christ is risen, God is here!

2. Christ has risen for the people
   Whom he died to love and save;
   Christ has risen for the women
   Bringing flowers to grace his grave.
   Christ has risen for disciples
   Huddled in an upstairs room.
   He whose word inspired creation
   Can't be silenced by the tomb.

3. Christ has risen to companion
   Former friends who fear the night,
   Sensing loss and limitation
   Where their faith had once burned bright.
   They bemoan what is no longer,
   They expect no hopeful sign
   Till Christ ends their conversation,
   Breaking bread and sharing wine.

4. Christ has risen and forever
   Lives to challenge and to change
   All whose lives are messed or mangled,
   All who find religion strange.
   Christ is risen. Christ is present
   Making us what he has been —
   Evidence of transformation
   In which God is known and seen.

This gentler Easter song is easily learned. It need not be taught in advance. If different solo voices sing the first three verses, perhaps from different parts of the building or next to different symbols of the resurrection, everyone will be able to join in verse 4.

DARKNESS IS GONE

Tune: DAYLIGHT (JLB)

joyfully

Dark—ness is gone, _____ day-light has come: _____ the

Son of God and man a—ri—ses with the dawn.__ Death

lo—ses its sin-i-ster sting: ___ God's pro-mise to do a new thing is

done, and Hal-le—lu——jah! earth joins heaven to sing._____

Words and Music © 1988 The Iona Community

1. Darkness is gone, daylight has come:
   The Son of God and man arises with the dawn.
   Death loses its sinister sting:
   God's promise to do a new thing
   Is done, and Hallelujah!
   Earth joins heaven to sing.

2. See now the cross, see now the grave:
   They, vacant, celebrate how God's foolishness can save.
   The criminal nailed as a fraud
   Is raised by the power of God
   And lives. So, Hallelujah!
   Scatter the news abroad.

3. Greener the grass, brighter the sun,
   The God-loved world proclaims a new age has begun.
   Creation is decked for her guest
   Who, freed from his grave clothes is dressed
   In light and, Hallelujah!
   Tells that the earth is blessed.

4. The needed trust, the longed-for peace
   Are passed as hands from sword and shackle are released.
   The violence of hate reigns no more:
   The victory of love is the core
   Of hope and, Hallelujah!
   Love means an open door.

5. "The Kingdom comes!" the King proclaims:
   Justice and joy abound where Christ-filled faith pertains.
   Religion, remote and typecast,
   Is gone and the future is vast.
   New tongues sing, "Hallelujah!
     God is for us at last!"

6. Enrol the drum, enlist the gong
   To celebrate in sound that right has conquered wrong.
   Join hands with the neighbour unknown,
   Unite through the love that is shown
   In Christ, for, Hallelujah!
   He is our Lord alone.

Only sing all six verses when the song is being used as a recessional —
which was its original intention. To shorten it, stop at verse 5, or omit
verses 4 and 5. This song should be sung in unison.

THE LORD OF ALL

Tune: LORD OF ALL (JLB)

at a lively pace

The Bread of Life, the car-pen-ter's own son,_____ has made a

Dmaj7   Dm7

feast and calls us to his ta-ble. His food is sim — ple and his words are

Em7   A7   D   Dmaj7

plain; his guests need neith-er sta-tus, rank nor la-bel. HE IS THE

Dm7   Em7   A7   D

LORD OF ALL THAT IS AND ALL THAT IS TO BE, _____ AND OF ME. SO LET YOUR HANDS MEET MINE AND SHARE THE BREAD AND WINE THAT SETS US FREE. _____ vv. 1-3. He is the v.4. THAT SETS US FREE. _____

rallentando

Gmaj7   A7/G   Fm7

Bm7   Em7   C

A   G/A

Bb   Gm7   D

Words and Music © 1988 The Iona Community

1.   The Bread of Life, the carpenter's own son,
      Has made a feast and calls us to his table.
      His food is simple and his words are plain;
      His guests need neither status, rank nor label.

Chorus : HE IS THE LORD OF ALL THAT IS
            AND ALL THAT IS TO BE,
            AND OF ME.
            SO LET YOUR HANDS MEET MINE
            AND SHARE THE BREAD AND WINE
            THAT SETS US FREE.   *(repeat for last chorus)*

2.   He is the Alpha and the Omega,
      The King of Love and thus the Prince of Peace.
      What he begins shall never need an end:
      The life he lives is never meant to cease.

3.   He is the Servant suffering for our wrong
      And yet the Lord who dances on the grave.
      He helps the weak assist the very strong
      And gives the poor the dignity they crave.

4.   Each beating heart, each body and each mind
      Are summoned still to answer to his call.
      Whoever yearns for something greater yet
      Shall find in Christ the answer and the all.

Ideally this song should be sung at an Easter Communion, but its use is restricted to neither Easter nor sacramental occasions. By substituting for the last two lines of the chorus the words:
            TO SHARE A SIGN THAT CHRIST
            HAS SET US FREE.
– the song may be more easily used in situations where communion is not being celebrated.

At all times it should be sung with a lively tempo.

EASTER EVENING

Tune: THE SILKIE (Scottish Trad.)

gently

As we walked home at close of day, a

strang — er joined us on our way. He

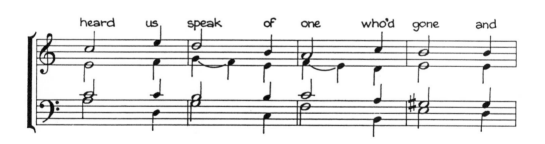

heard us speak of one who'd gone and

when we stopped, he carr——ied on.

Words and Arrangement © 1988 The Iona Community

1. As we walked home at close of day,
   A stranger joined us on our way.
   He heard us speak of one who'd gone
   And when we stopped, he carried on.

2. "Why wander further without light?
   Please stay with us this troubled night.
   We've shared the truth of how we feel
   And now would like to share a meal."

3. We sat to eat our simple spread,
   Then watched the stranger take the bread;
   And, as he said the blessing prayer,
   We knew that someone else was there.

4. No stranger he; it was our eyes
   Which failed to see, in stranger's guise,
   The Lord who, risen from the dead,
   Met us when ready to be fed.

5. Alleluia! Alleluia!
   Alleluia! Alleluia!
   As Mary and our sisters said,
   The Lord is risen from the dead!

The very haunting tune enables this song to be sung with an air of
mystery. Let one or two people sing verse 2 while the harmony is
hummed beneath them.

HE COMES

Tune: HE COMES (JLB)

at a slow bluesy pace

He comes_____ in the gath-er-ing gloom: _____ a

man_____ to a dark up-stairs room. _____ He

meets_____ with his friends and he breaks _____ bread he

Words and Music © 1988 The Iona Community

takes. _____ *Fine.* SO,

PRAISE THE LORD FOR WORD AND SIGN THAT AT HIS FEAST WE'RE

CALLED TO DINE, AND PRAISE THE LORD FOR BREAD AND WINE THROUGH

WHICH HE SAYS, 'YOU ALL ARE MINE.' *D.C.*

1. He comes, in the gathering gloom:
    A man to a dark upstairs room.
    He meets with his friends and he breaks
    Bread he takes.

Chorus : SO, PRAISE THE LORD FOR WORD AND SIGN
            THAT AT HIS FEAST WE'RE CALLED TO DINE,
            AND PRAISE THE LORD FOR BREAD AND WINE
            THROUGH WHICH HE SAYS, "YOU ALL ARE MINE."

2. He comes, at the close of the day:
    The stranger who's going our way.
    He joins us at table for food:
    He is good.

3. He comes, to stand outside our door:
    The king of the rich and the poor.
    He waits to be shown to his seat
    And to eat.

4. He comes, at the end of all time
    To call, to his banquet sublime,
    The faithful, both living and dead,
    As he said.

5. He comes as the host and the guest;
    He comes in the bread which is blest;
    He comes, in the wine which is new,
    Just for you.

The table is where Jesus met, and still meets, his friends. So this song depicts several instances in the Bible where Jesus is known to be with his people.

The bluesy verses should have preferably a female soloist and end after verse five without the chorus, thus giving, if required, a fitting introduction to a celebration of Holy Communion.

OPEN THE DOOR

Tune: KNOCKING (JLB)

with excitement

O-PEN THE DOOR: HE'S KNOCK—ING! O-PEN THE DOOR: HE'S KNOCK—ING!

JE-SUS IS KNOCK — ING! JE-SUS IS KNOCK—ING!

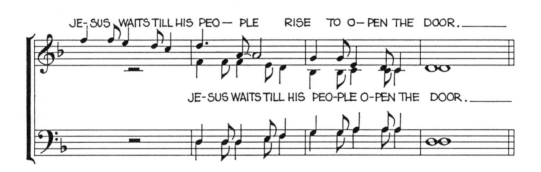

JE-SUS WAITS TILL HIS PEO — PLE RISE TO O-PEN THE DOOR._____

JE-SUS WAITS TILL HIS PEO-PLE O-PEN THE DOOR._____

With half the world hung—ry,_____ we've food on our ta — ble._____

With half the world hung — ry, we've food on our

We know we could share it _____ but think we're un — a — ble. ____

ta — ble. We wish we could share it. Oh _____

(solo voice) It's no-thing to dis-turb us! It's just the child-ren play-ing!

WHAT'S THAT NOISE? WHO'S OUT THERE?

It's your im-ag-in-a-tion! Fine.

WHAT'S THAT NOISE? SOME-ONE'S KNOCK — ING.

Words and Music © 1988 The Iona Community

Chorus : OPEN THE DOOR: HE'S KNOCKING!
OPEN THE DOOR: HE'S KNOCKING!
JESUS WAITS TILL HIS PEOPLE
RISE TO OPEN THE DOOR.

1.   With half the world hungry,
     We've food on our table.
     We know we could share it
     But think we're unable.

     WHAT'S THAT NOISE?   . . . It's nothing to disturb us!
     WHO'S OUT THERE?   . . . It's just the children playing!
     WHAT'S THAT NOISE?   . . . It's your imagination!
     SOMEONE'S KNOCKING!

2.   The company we're part of
     Knows no deprivation;
     It's those we keep waiting,
     Without invitation.

3.   The love that unites us
     Is always in danger
     Of failing to welcome
     The hesitant stranger.

4.   He waits and he wonders,
     But won't analyse us.
     He's brought bread and wine to
     Refresh and surprise us.

A four-part choir is necessary to give this song its best effect. The choir sings the verses and the refrain with a solo respondent during each verse. The song ends, not with the positive chorus, but the incompleteness of the refrain.

JESUS CHRIST IS WAITING

Tune: NOEL NOUVELET (French Trad.)

brightly

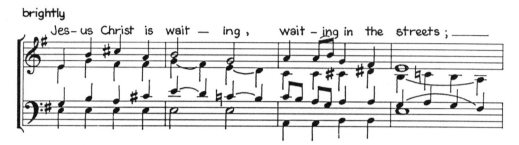

Jes-us Christ is wait — ing, wait-ing in the streets; _____

no-one is his neigh — bour, all a — lone he eats. _____

Lis — ten, Lord Je — sus, I am lone-ly too. _____

Make me, friend or stran — ger, fit to wait on you. _____

Words and Arrangement © 1988 The Iona Community

1. Jesus Christ is waiting,
   Waiting in the streets;
   No one is his neighbour,
   All alone he eats.
   Listen, Lord Jesus,
   I am lonely too.
   Make me, friend or stranger,
   Fit to wait on you.

2. Jesus Christ is raging,
   Raging in the streets,
   Where injustice spirals
   And real hope retreats.
   Listen, Lord Jesus,
   I am angry too.
   In the Kingdom's causes
   Let me rage with you.

3. Jesus Christ is healing,
   Healing in the streets;
   Curing those who suffer,
   Touching those he greets.
   Listen, Lord Jesus,
   I have pity too.
   Let my care be active,
   Healing just like you.

4. Jesus Christ is dancing,
   Dancing in the streets,
   Where each sign of hatred
   He, with love, defeats.
   Listen, Lord Jesus,
   I should triumph too.
   On suspicion's graveyard
   Let me dance with you.

5. Jesus Christ is calling,
   Calling in the streets,
   "Who will join my journey?
    I will guide their feet."
   Listen, Lord Jesus,
   Let my fears be few.
   Walk one step before me;
   I will follow you.

The tune *Noel Nouvelet* has immediate associations with Easter and makes it a fitting match to these words. The mood of each verse should be different — something which can be aided by skilful playing on hand drums.

GO HOME BY ANOTHER WAY

Tune: BROTHER KEITH (JLB)

with a lively tempo

Once you've seen the ba-by in the man-ger, will you go to tell the jeal-ous

G   Am7   D7   G

king? Will you trade the safe-ty of the Sav-iour,

Am7   D7   Bm7   Em

sell your soul and ru—in eve—ry—thing?_____

Am7   Bm7   Em

Harmony. GO HOME, GO HOME, GO

GO HOME, GO HOME, GO

Am7   D   Gmaj7   C

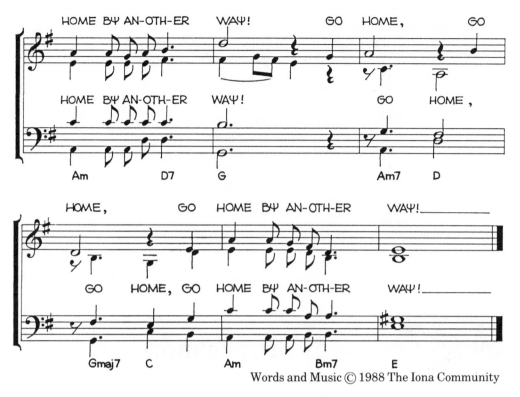

1. Once you've seen the baby in the manger,
   Will you go to tell the jealous king?
   Will you trade the safety of the Saviour,
   Sell your soul and ruin everything?

   Chorus :   GO HOME, GO HOME,
   GO HOME BY ANOTHER WAY!
   GO HOME, GO HOME,
   GO HOME BY ANOTHER WAY!

2. Once you've heard the teacher in the temple,
   Will you take offence at what he says?
   Will you call him saved and yet misguided
   When he claims that profit seldom pays?

3. When you feel the handshake of the healer,
   Will you let him take your deepest pain?
   Will you dare release the hurt you're feeling
   Or ensure his interest is in vain?

4. When you taste the wine from heaven's waiter,
   Will you celebrate his presence here?
   Will you shout with joy instead of anger
   Or suspect God's presence in good cheer?

5. When you smell the death of the redeemer,
    Will you realise he died for you?
    Will you see that suffering and forgiving
    Are the work of grace he came to do?

6. When you know that Jesus Christ is risen,
    Will you carry on as if he's dead?
    Will you recognise that love has triumphed,
    Hell has lost and Heaven is here instead?

It is not only the Wise Men who had to change their way after meeting
Jesus, but everyone who wanted to take him seriously. Though this
song deals with the five senses, there is no need to sing all the verses.

THE SORROW

Tune: REALITY (JLB)

Don't tell me of a faith that fears to face the world a-round; Don't
dull my mind with eas-y thoughts of grace with-out a ground. I
NEED TO KNOW THAT GOD IS REAL! I NEED TO KNOW THAT CHRIST CAN FEEL THE
NEED TO TOUCH AND LOVE AND HEAL THE WORLD, IN-CLUD-ING ME!

Words and Music © 1988 The Iona Community

1. Don't tell me of a faith that fears
    To face the world around;
    Don't dull my mind with easy thoughts
    Of grace without a ground.

Chorus : I NEED TO KNOW THAT GOD IS REAL!
            I NEED TO KNOW THAT CHRIST CAN FEEL
            THE NEED TO TOUCH AND LOVE AND HEAL
            THE WORLD, INCLUDING ME!

2. Don't speak of piety and prayers
    Absolved from human need;
    Don't talk of spirit without flesh
    Like harvest without seed.

3. Don't sate my soul with common sense
    Distilled from ages past,
    Inept for those who fear the world's
    About to breathe its last.

4. Don't set the cross before my eyes
    Unless you tell the truth
    Of how the Lord, who finds the lost,
    Was often found uncouth.

5. So, let the Gospel come alive,
    In actions plain to see
    In imitation of the one
    Whose love extends to me.

A protest song about bogus religion might well suit the Sunday after Easter, when Jesus appeared to Thomas. Now, as then, people should be able to cry for a faith which is real and relevant, satisfied only by a Lord who lives on both sides of the grave.

Have the verses sung solo . . . all by one person or each by a different person.

SHOW YOUR FACE

Tune: UP IN THE MORNIN' EARLY (Scottish Trad.)

brightly

The Word of Life and Lord of Love, God's chos—en and our choos——er, has made his home am——ong the poor and sid——ed with the los———er. THEN SHOW YOUR FACE AND TAKE YOUR PLACE, AND SHARE YOUR TIME AND TREAS—URE WHERE NO ONE LESS THAN CHRIST THE KING TAKES RE—FUGE AND BRINGS PLEAS—URE.

1.   The Word of Life and Lord of Love,
     God's chosen and our chooser,
     Has made his home among the poor
     And sided with the loser.

Chorus :   THEN SHOW YOUR FACE AND TAKE YOUR PLACE,
             AND SHARE YOUR TIME AND TREASURE
             WHERE NO ONE LESS THAN CHRIST THE KING
             TAKES REFUGE AND BRINGS PLEASURE.

2.   Unqualified and out of work,
     In simple clothes he dresses;
     He dines with those the world discards,
     His love their hurt caresses.

3.   He speaks of God in children's terms,
     He tells domestic stories,
     He walks to heaven on earth's byeways,
     Religious folk he worries.

4.   A fish, a loaf, a seed, a coin,
     A cup, a cross, a silence,
     An empty tomb, an upstairs room −
     By these he conquers violence.

5.   In pain, redundancy and loss,
     In stigma and rejection,
     The Son of God is present yet,
     Inspiring resurrection.

The title of the tune makes it appropriate for a post-resurrection hymn. As with other folk tunes, it is often easy to get people singing if you have one person singing the first verse and chorus, two singing the second and gradually add the others as they become familiar with the tune.

CHRIST IN THE STRANGER'S GUISE

Tune: THE LEAVING OF LIVERPOOL (Irish Trad.)

brightly

From heaven to here and from here to heaven is a dist-ance less than tis-sue

thin, _____ and it's trod by him who, in the stran-ger's guise, is made

known when he is wel-comed in. _____ SO, COME LORD CHRIST IN THE

STRAN — GER'S GUISE, KNOWN BOTH THROUGH SCRIP-TURES AND THROUGH BRO-KEN

BREAD. YOUR KING-DOM COME AND ON THE EARTH YOUR WILL BE DONE BY THE

PEO — PLE YOU'VE LOVED AND YOU'VE LED. _____

Words © 1988 The Iona Community

1. From heaven to here and from here to heaven
    Is a distance less than tissue thin,
    And it's trod by him who, in the stranger's guise,
    Is made known when he is welcomed in.

Chorus :
    SO, COME LORD CHRIST IN THE STRANGER'S GUISE,
    KNOWN BOTH THROUGH SCRIPTURES AND THROUGH BROKEN BREAD.
    YOUR KINGDOM COME AND ON THE EARTH YOUR WILL BE DONE
    BY THE PEOPLE YOU'VE LOVED AND YOU'VE LED.

2. The folk who journey on the road with Christ
    Are the ones who've left their selves behind.
    Their song is taught them by the deaf and dumb;
    Their horizon is shown by the blind.

3. The love that's shared along the royal road
    Is a love not found when standing still.
    It lives and grows wherever faith is known
    As a movement grounded in God's will.

4. From heaven to here and from here to heaven
    Is a distance less than tissue thin,
    And it's trod by those who meet the risen Christ
    As a stranger to be welcomed in.

The image of Christ as the 'stranger' is constant throughout the Gospels. It is as a stranger that he meets his disciples after the resurrection, thus requiring the infant church to be always open to the outsider.

BE STILL AND KNOW

Tune: BE STILL (JLB)

very gently

Be still and know that I am God, AND

THERE IS NONE BE-SIDE ME. _____ BE STILL AND KNOW THAT

I AM GOD,   AND THERE IS NONE BE-SIDE ME. _____

1. *Cantor*: Be still and know that I am God,
   All   : AND THERE IS NONE BESIDE ME.
              BE STILL AND KNOW THAT I AM GOD,
              AND THERE IS NONE BESIDE ME.

   Voice : The greatest love a person can have for his friends is to give his life
   for them. And you are my friends if you do what I command you.

   I do not call you servants, because a servant does not know what his
   master is doing. But I have told you everything I heard from my
   Father . . . so I call you my friends.

2. *Cantor*: I am the one who calls you my friends,
   All   : AND THERE IS NONE BESIDE ME . . .   *(as above)*
   Voice : If you obey my commands, you will know my love, just as I have
   obeyed my Father's commands and know his love. And my
   command is simply that you love each other as I have loved you. I
   chose you, and I have appointed you to go and bear much fruit –
   the kind that will last.

   But remember, I chose you – you did not choose me.

3. *Cantor*: I am the one whose love never fails,
   All   : *(as above)*
   Voice : Those who love their own life will lose it.
   Those who do not love their own life in this world
           will keep it forever.
   Those who want to serve me must follow me.
   Whoever follows me I will never turn away.

4. *Cantor*: I am the one who says "Follow me",
   All   : *(as above)*
   Voice : When he came down to earth at Bethlehem,
           he came down . . . alone.
   When he ran away from his parents, he ran away . . . alone.
   When he was tempted in the desert, he was tempted . . . alone.
   When he was brought before Pilate, he was brought . . . alone.
   When he was crucified and buried, he rose again . . . alone.
   For there is none better than him,
             none above him,
             none beside him.

5. *Cantor*: Be still and know that I am God,
   All   : *(as above)*

This meditation requires someone to read the words between the
verses. Simple chords played or strummed under the voice help to keep
the unity of the song.

THE SAVIOUR LEAVES

Tune: ASCENSION (JLB)

majestically

For-sak-ing char-iots of fire

and fan-fared brass, as strange-ly sil-ent as he came,

the Sav-iour leaves and God, with heavens ca-ress, the Son re-

1. Forsaking chariots of fire
   And fanfared brass,
   As strangely silent as he came,
   The Saviour leaves
   And God, with heaven's caress,
   The Son receives.

2. He has to go, as from the grave
   He had to rise:
   In order to be everywhere
   He must depart
   To live, not in one place,
   But in each heart.

3. So, Christ ascends; air cradles him,
   Disciples stare.
   Their Easter joy, his seven week's stay
   Seem now to end.
   But no! The Spirit's sending
   They portend.

4. Let angel harmonies resound;
   Let trumpets blare;
   Let heaven's banquet guests applaud
   The welcomed Word,
   And earth anticipate
   Her coming Lord.

This may seem to be not for the faint-hearted, but it really is quite easy to sing. For maximum effect an organ is required for the accompaniment.

THE LAST JOURNEY

Tune: IONA BOAT SONG (Scottish Trad.)

slowly and reverently

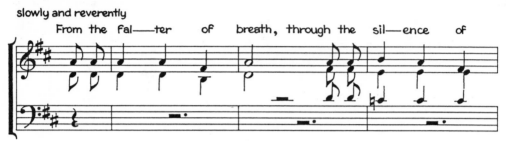

From the fal—ter of breath, through the sil—ence of

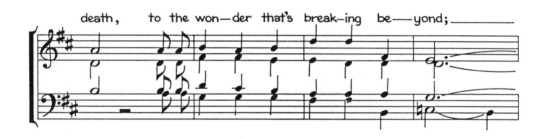

death, to the won—der that's break—ing be—yond;

God has wov—en a way, un—ap—par—ent by

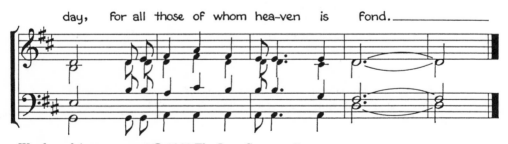

day, for all those of whom hea—ven is fond.

1. From the falter of breath,
   Through the silence of death,
   To the wonder that's breaking beyond;
   God has woven a way,
   Unapparent by day,
   For all those of whom heaven is fond.

2. From frustration and pain,
   Through hope hard to sustain,
   To the wholeness here promised, there known;
   Christ has gone where we fear
   And has vowed to be near
   On the journey we make on our own.

3. From the dimming of light,
   Through the darkness of night,
   To the glory of goodness above;
   God the Spirit is sent
   To ensure heaven's intent
   Is embraced and completed in love.

4. From today till we die,
   Through all questioning why,
   To the place from which time and tide flow;
   Angels tread on our dreams
   And magnificent themes
   Of heaven's promise are echoed below.

Legend has it that this tune was used as ancient Scottish kings were, after death, rowed to their resting place on the island of Iona. It would be a pity if such a fine tune were reserved solely for the use of royalty.

The song is best sung unaccompanied, whether in unison or four parts.

THE HOLY SPIRIT, COMING TO STAY

COME, HOLY SPIRIT

Tune: VENI, SANCTE SPIRITUS (JLB)

gently

(Desc.) Come, ___ Ho — ly Spi — rit; _____ come, ___ Heav-en-ly Dove; _____
come, __ Source of Re-new-al ; _____ come , preg-nant with love. _____

VE — NI, SANC —TE SPIR —IT-US, _____ VE — NI, SANC —TE SPIR — IT-US. _____

a little quicker

Speak , speak to our sad-ness, _____ Christ's word of re-lease ; _____

plant   seeds for our free-dom , ___ clear   path-ways for peace . ___ D.C.

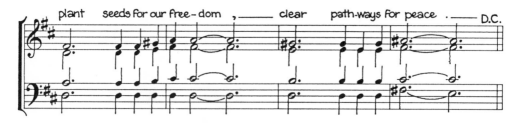

Chorus : VENI, SANCTE SPIRITUS,
VENI, SANCTE SPIRITUS,
VENI, SANCTE SPIRITUS,
VENI, SANCTE SPIRITUS.

(Repeat with Descant)

Descant : Come, Holy Spirit;
Come, Heavenly Dove;
Come, Source of Renewal;
Come, pregnant with love.

1.   Speak, speak to our sadness,
Christ's word of release;
Plant seeds for our freedom,
Clear pathways for peace.

(Chorus with descant after each verse)

2.   Find, find in our lostness,
True signs of our worth,
Raw proof of the saltness
Sent, meant for the earth.

3.   Fire, fire in the darkness,
New flame for the soul;
Light lamps for our growing
From broken to whole.

To sing this effectively, a small group should take the verses, everyone sing the chorus and three or four high female voices sing the descant.

PENTECOST

Tune: ST. JOHN'S, GOUROCK (JLB)

brightly

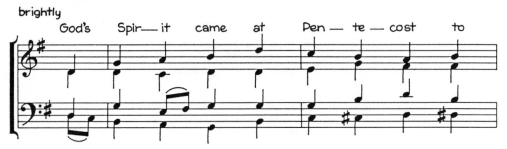

God's Spir—it came at Pen—te—cost to

folk who thought their faith was lost; in-spired by wind and

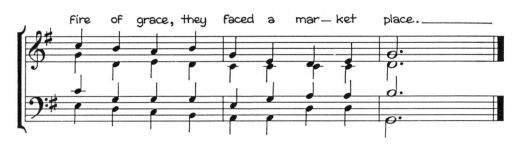

fire of grace, they faced a mar—ket place._____

1. God's Spirit came at Pentecost
   To folk who feared their faith was lost;
   Inspired by wind and fire of grace,
   They faced a market place.

2. And there, in tongues they'd never known,
   They preached the Gospel Christ had shown.
   Some scorned the depths to which they'd sunk;
   Some laughed and called them drunk.

3. Despite the jeers, amidst the scorn,
   The Holy Catholic Church was born,
   Fulfilling what the prophets said
   And following where Christ led.

4. The multi-racial audience heard
   What God, through the apostles, said;
   And many, who had come to mock,
   Stayed to believe and talk.

5. Even now, as in the earliest day,
   We feel uncertain. Yet we pray:
   Lord, shake and stir your Church again
   Till noticed like drunk men.

6. Thus may the God of all be blessed;
   Thus may Christ's Gospel be confessed;
   Thus may the Spirit, where we meet,
   Bless sanctuary and street.

This song is in 8886 metre. Appropriate alternative tunes are *Childhood* and *Saffron Walden*.

GOD THE SPIRIT COMES TO STAY

Tune: McALOON (JLB)

very calmly

GOD THE SPI—RIT COMES TO STAY.

Words and Music © 1988 The Iona Community

1. If you would love me, keep my commandments.
    Then shall my Father send down from heaven
    One who reveals the Truth you obey.

    Chorus : JESUS, ASCENDED,
                KEEPS TO HIS PROMISE:
                GOD THE SPIRIT COMES TO STAY.

2. This is the seed and source of creation;
    None can receive him unless they know me.
    Thus he is yours who follow my way.

3. Though I go from you, still I am with you.
    Blind though the world is, yet you will see me;
    God will confirm whatever I say.

4. Peace I leave with you; my peace I give you.
    Don't let your hearts be troubled or weary.
    Help is at hand whenever you pray.

The words are a paraphrase of Jesus' promise of the Spirit found in
John chapter 14. It is a gentle song for Holy Week as well as Pentecost.
For good effect, a solo voice could take the verses with everyone
humming their parts underneath, and all singing the chorus.

HEAVEN ON EARTH

Tune: HO RI HO RO (A. Sinclair)

brightly

THE GOD OF HEAVEN IS PRES-ENT ON EARTH IN

WORD AND SIL-ENCE AND SHAR—ING, IN FACE OF DOUBT, IN

DEPTH OF FAITH, IN SIGNS OF LOVE AND CAR——ING. *Fine.*

Gent ler—than air, wild—er than wind,

sett—ling yet al—so de-rang——ing, the Spi-rit thrives in

hu——man lives both chang-less and yet chang——ing. *D.C.*

Chorus : THE GOD OF HEAVEN IS PRESENT ON EARTH
IN WORD AND SILENCE AND SHARING,
IN FACE OF DOUBT, IN DEPTH OF FAITH,
IN SIGNS OF LOVE AND CARING.

1. Gentler than air, wilder than wind,
Settling yet also deranging,
The Spirit thrives in human lives
Both changeless and yet changing.

2. Far from the church, outside the fold,
Where prayer turns feeble and nervous,
The Spirit wills society's ills
Be healed through humble service.

3. From country quiet to city riot,
In every human confusion,
The Spirit pleads for all that leads
To freedom from illusion.

4. Truth after tears, trust after fears,
God after all that denies him:
The Spirit springs through hopeless things
Transforming what defies him.

If there is, in your church, a dance group or even a group of people
willing to move their bodies to music, this is a good song to interpret in
simple actions.

ENEMY OF APATHY

Tune: THAINAKY (JLB)

not too quickly

She sits like a bird,

Em   Bm7   Em   Bm7   Em

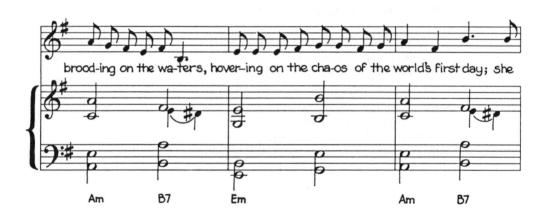

brood-ing on the wa-ters, hover-ing on the cha-os of the world's first day; she

Am   B7   Em   Am   B7

sighs and she sings, moth-er-ing cre-a-tion, wait-ing to give birth to all the

Am7   D7   Gmaj7   Cmaj7   Fmaj7   Am7

114

Word will say.

B   Em   Bm7   Em   Bm7   E

last time.

1. She sits like a bird, brooding on the waters,
   Hovering on the chaos of the world's first day;
   She sighs and she sings, mothering creation,
   Waiting to give birth to all the Word will say.

2. She wings over earth, resting where she wishes,
   Lighting close at hand or soaring through the skies;
   She nests in the womb, welcoming each wonder,
   Nourishing potential hidden to our eyes.

3. She dances in fire, startling her spectators,
   Waking tongues of ecstasy where dumbness reigned;
   She weans and inspires all whose hearts are open,
   Nor can she be captured, silenced or restrained.

4. For she is the Spirit, one with God in essence,
   Gifted by the Saviour in eternal love;
   She is the key opening the scriptures,
   Enemy of apathy and heavenly dove.

In Hebrew, the word used for the Spirit is *ruach* . . . a feminine noun. Genesis Chapter 1 and Psalm 139 are two passages of scripture which speak of the Spirit in female images. These are reflected in this song.

At first, it may seem strange to use the pronoun 'she', but that is the fault both of the English language and of masculine-oriented theology which fails to grasp the liberating significance of Paul's comment that in Jesus Christ 'there is neither male nor female'.

THE LOVE OF GOD COMES CLOSE

Tune: MELANIE (JLB)

gently

The love of God comes

close   where stands an op——en door

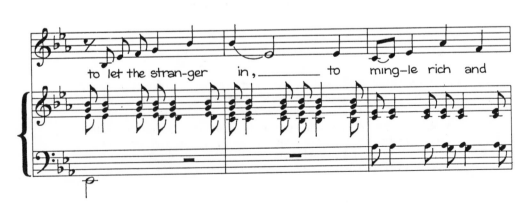

to let the stran-ger   in, ————— to   ming-le rich and

poor:_____ the love of God is here to stay em-brac-ing those who

walk his way._____

1. The love of God comes close
   Where stands an open door
   To let the stranger in,
   To mingle rich and poor:
   The love of God is here to stay
   Embracing those who walk his way.

2. The peace of God comes close
   To those caught in the storm,
   Forgoing lives of ease
   To ease the lives forlorn:
   The peace of God is here to stay
   Embracing those who walk his way.

3. The joy of God comes close
   Where faith encounters fears,
   Where heights and depths of life
   Are found through smiles and tears:
   The joy of God is here to stay
   Embracing those who walk his way.

4. The grace of God comes close
   To those whose grace is spent,
   When hearts are tired or sore
   And hope is bruised or bent:
   The grace of God is here to stay
   Embracing those who walk his way.

5. The Son of God comes close
   Where people praise his name,
   Where bread and wine are blest
   And shared, as when he came:
   The Son of God is here to stay
   Embracing those who walk his way.

When using this tune, subdivide the group so that not all sing at the
same time until the final verse. An alternative tune in the same metre
is *Love Unknown*. Where Communion is not being celebrated, verse 5
may be omitted.

LO, I AM WITH YOU

Tune: PRESENCE (JLB)

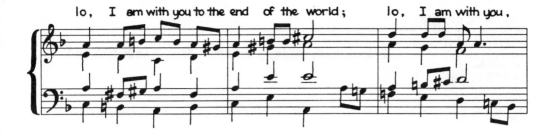

Words and Music © 1988 The Iona Community

1. Lo, I am with you to the end of the world;
   Lo, I am with you to the end of the world;
   Lo, I am with you,
   Lo, I am with you,
   Lo, I am with you to the end of the world.

2. Lo, I am with you when you leave self behind . . .

3. Lo, I am with you in the struggle for peace . . .

4. Lo, I am with you when you suffer for love . . .

5. Lo, I am with you in the way of the cross . . .

6. Lo, I am with you in the darkness of death . . .

7. Lo, I am with you to the end of the world . . .

Because of the simplicity of the words, it is often enough, when singing this song without accompaniment, to have a cantor sing the first line of each verse. This song should be sung in unison.

People may want to improvise additional verses of their own. Or it might be appropriate to use the themes of the verses to focus intercession, singing the appropriate verse after each section of prayers.

NO ONE WILL EVER BE THE SAME

Tune: ROYSTONHILL (JLB)

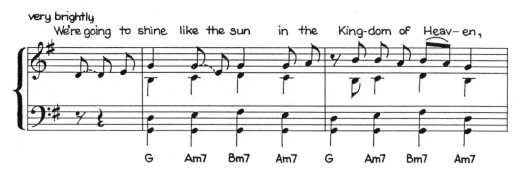

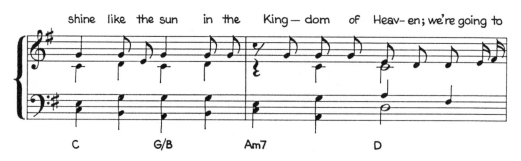

1. *Cantor* : We're going to shine like the sun in the Kingdom of Heaven,

    All : Shine like the sun in the Kingdom of Heaven;
    We're going to shine like the sun in the Kingdom of Heaven
    And no one will ever be the same.

    Chorus : AND IT'S ALL IN JESUS' NAME;
    AND IT'S ALL IN JESUS' NAME;
    YES IT'S ALL IN JESUS' NAME
    THAT NO ONE WILL EVER BE THE SAME.

2. *Cantor* : We're going to learn from the poor in the Kingdom of Heaven,

    All : *(as above)*

3. *Cantor* : We're going to walk with the weak in the Kingdom of Heaven, ...

4. *Cantor* : We're going to drink new wine in the Kingdom of Heaven, ...

5. *Cantor* : And it all starts now in the Kingdom of Heaven, ...

This is a good recessional song, especially as people leave joyfully from church after communion. Here it is suggested that a cantor sings the first line of each verse, but the whole verse may equally well be sung by everyone. With such simple words, there is no need for people to sing or move with heads buried in books.

O BLESS THE LORD

Tune: O BLESS THE LORD (JLB)

brightly

O, my soul, O, my

O, bless the Lord, o, bless the Lord,

soul, bless the Lord and nev-er for-get his

o, bless the Lord, bless the Lord and nev-er for-get his

love! O, my soul, O, my

love! O, bless the Lord, o, bless the Lord,

soul, bless the Lord and nev-er for-get his love!

o, bless the Lord, bless the Lord and nev-er for-get his love!

Chorus   :   O BLESS THE LORD, O MY SOUL,
O BLESS THE LORD, O MY SOUL,
O BLESS THE LORD,
BLESS THE LORD AND NEVER FORGET HIS LOVE !
O BLESS THE LORD, O MY SOUL,
O BLESS THE LORD, O MY SOUL,
O BLESS THE LORD,
BLESS THE LORD AND NEVER FORGET HIS LOVE !

Verse   : His name is Wonderful;
His name is Counsellor;
His name is Prince of Peace
Whose Kingdom shall have no end.
He is the Mighty God;
He is the Lord of Hosts;
He is the King of Heaven,
Our Saviour, Our God and Friend.

Chorus   :   O BLESS THE LORD, O MY SOUL . . .

                    (As above . . .)

Two voices at least are required for this song. Half the group can take the bass part and half the soprano line if there are not enough to sing four-part harmony.

The words from Isaiah chapter 9 are normally associated with Christmas, but are broad enough to be used at any time. in the Christian Year to celebrate the magnificence of God.

PAUL'S SONG

Tune: A ROSEBUD (Scottish Trad.)

Should I re-hearse with hu—man voice the words which

an—gels make their choice, de—void of love, my

song re—sounds mag—ni—fi—cent but emp—ty. And

should I preach with earn—est tone and know what—

124

ev — er   can   be   known   and   move   the   hills   by

faith   a — lone — if   I   lack   love, I'm   noth———ing.

1. Should I rehearse with human voice
   The words which angels make their choice,
   Devoid of love, my song resounds
   Magnificent but empty.
   And should I preach with earnest tone
   And know whatever can be known
   And move the hills by faith alone —
   If I lack love, I'm nothing.

2. In love is patience always found,
   For love kind hearts make common ground,
   From love, conceit and pride take flight
   And jealousy is banished.
   Love keeps no score of what's gone wrong
   Nor sings a pessimistic song
   Nor lets regret or guilt prolong,
   For love expects tomorrow.

3.   Let strange and startling language cease,
      Let tongues their ecstasy release,
      Let knowledge come and go in peace —
      These things are not eternal.
      For all the thought and skill we show
      Are but a stage through which we grow
      Till, face to face with God, we'll know
      That love which lasts forever.

This paraphrase of 1st Corinthians chapter 13 is set to a tune which, typical of many Scottish folk tunes, has a very wide range. It may therefore be helpful to sing it a tone or semi-tone lower if being used with a large group of people with mixed vocal abilities.

CHANTS AND RESPONSES

MEDITATIVE CHANTS AND RESPONSES

The chants included here, though based on Easter themes, need not be restricted to that season, but can be used throughout the year.

Below are some suggestions as to how each might be used.

BEHOLD THE LAMB OF GOD

BEHOLD THE LAMB OF GOD,
BEHOLD THE LAMB OF GOD.
HE TAKES AWAY THE SIN,
THE SIN OF THE WORLD.

This may be used as a meditative song while the elements of bread and wine are being shared at Holy Communion, or it might be sung at the beginning of all services during Lent, when our attention is drawn to the path Jesus takes to the cross.

Another use, especially in a small group, is to get people to think about their favourite picture of Jesus. This should be a genuine biblical picture, rather than an artist's impression. One at a time they say what they see and, after each contribution, the chant is sung. It is best if everyone agrees to start with the same simple formula: − "He's . . . ."

e.g. "He's sitting in the middle of a crowd of men and he's picking up a little child to sit her on his knee."

"He's going up to a well to speak to a woman who has a terrible reputation. He's asking her for a cup of water."

OCCULI NOSTRI

OCCULI NOSTRI AD DOMINUM DEUM JESUM.
OCCULI NOSTRI AD DOMINUM NOSTRUM, SEMPER.

GOD KEEP OUR EYES FIXED ON JESUS, OUR LORD AND SAVIOUR.
GOD KEEP OUR EYES FIXED ON JESUS, OUR SAVIOUR, ALWAYS.

This chant can be used for the same purposes as the above.

A variation would be to write in advance a short list of some of the significant events of Jesus' life, with just a sentence or two to each event. Different members of the congregation could read these and the response be sung after a short silence. Or, instead of words, slides or posters might be displayed, a different one for each singing.

WATCH AND PRAY

WATCH, WATCH AND PRAY: JESUS WILL KEEP TO HIS WORD.
WATCH, WATCH AND PRAY: JESUS WILL KEEP TO HIS WORD.

As a meditation, take the beatitudes or other similar words of Jesus in which he makes a pronouncement or promise. After each one, the response is sung. Alternatively the response can be used to end sections in a prayer.

KYRIE ELEISON

KYRIE ELEISON,   KYRIE ELEISON.

(Lord, have mercy)

This simple chant, using two Greek words which come from the earliest days of the church, can be used as a response during prayers of confession.

WONDER AND STARE

WONDER AND STARE; FEAR AND BEWARE:
HEAVEN AND HELL ARE CLOSE AT HAND.
GOD'S LIVING WORD, JESUS THE LORD,
FOLLOWS WHERE FAITH AND LOVE DEMAND.

This is definitely a song for Passion Sunday, Palm Sunday or Holy Week. In churches where it is customary or possible to have a cross carried in during or at the beginning of worship, an extra dimension is added to that activity if this chant accompanies it.

Or it may be that on Passion Sunday a cross might be assembled during the service, letting the various parts be brought to the front and hammered together while all sing these words.

Where the stations of the cross are being remembered, the chant can be used as people move from one station to another.

ALLELUIA

ALLELUIA! ALLELUIA! ALLELUIA! ALLELUIA!
ALLELUIA! ALLELUIA! ALLELUIA! ALLELUIA!

This is a good recessional for Easter Day, either after the midnight vigil or at the close of morning worship. Most of the congregation can sing the tune, and those who normally sing parts can add the harmony.

COME, HOLY SPIRIT

COME, HOLY SPIRIT,
      GRACIOUS HEAVENLY DOVE;
COME, FIRE OF LOVE.

A chant for Pentecost or for the beginning of services of healing, ordinations or commissionings. It is effective if accompanied either by the lighting of the church or room, or by the lighting of seven candles — that being the number of churches to which the Spirit addressed Jesus' words in the Book of Revelation.

HERE I STAND

HERE I STAND AT THE DOOR
AND KNOCK, AND KNOCK.
I WILL COME AND DINE
WITH THOSE WHO ASK ME IN.

This is best used at the beginning of worship and is especially suited to sacramental occasions. The chant is in three parts, which are very easy to learn and sing.

THE KENTIGERN SETTING

This setting of chants and responses for Holy Communion is named after the patron saint of Glasgow, in which city it was first used.

KYRIE

KYRIE ELEISON, KYRIE ELEISON,
KYRIE ELEISON, AMEN. AMEN. AMEN.

Sing during, or before, the prayer of confession.

SANCTUS and BENEDICTUS

HOLY, HOLY, HOLY LORD OF POWER AND MIGHT.
HEAVEN, EARTH, HEAVEN AND EARTH ARE FULL OF YOUR GLORY.
ALL GLORY TO YOUR NAME.   ALL GLORY TO YOUR NAME.

BLESSED, BLESSED IS HE WHO COMES IN THE NAME OF THE LORD.
BLESSED, BLESSED IS HE WHO COMES IN THE NAME OF THE LORD.
HOSANNA IN THE HIGHEST.   HOSANNA IN THE HIGHEST.

Sing during the prayer before the sacrament when the congregation on earth is encouraged to join the song of the saints in heaven.

AGNUS DEI

LAMB OF GOD,
YOU TAKE AWAY THE SIN OF THE WORLD.
HAVE MERCY UPON US.

LAMB OF GOD,
YOU TAKE AWAY THE SIN OF THE WORLD.
HAVE MERCY UPON US.

LAMB OF GOD,
YOU TAKE AWAY THE SIN OF THE WORLD.
GRANT US YOUR PEACE.

Sing after the bread and wine have been consecrated and declared to be the body and blood of the Lord.

****

N.B. These chants and responses were **never** meant to be sung with an accompaniment. Organs and pianos run the risk of dominating the singing of people as much as they offer the opportunity of leading it. It takes a while for people to get used to unaccompanied singing but, once they have started, they rarely want to go back.

BEHOLD THE LAMB OF GOD

OCCULI NOSTRI

WATCH AND PRAY

Words and Music © 1988 The Iona Community

KYRIE ELEISON

Music © 1988 The Iona Community

WONDER AND STARE

Hell are close at hand. God's liv—ing Word, Je—sus the

Lord, fol—lows where faith and love de—mand.

ALLELUIA

Al—le-lu-ia! AL-LE-LU-IA!_____ Al—le-lu-ia! AL-LE-LU-IA!_____

AL-LE-LU-IA! AL-LE-LU-IA!_____ AL—LE-LU—IA! AL-LE-LU-IA!_____

COME, HOLY SPIRIT

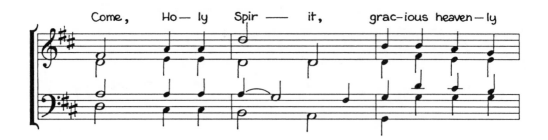

HERE I STAND

KENTIGERN SETTING

KYRIE

Music © 1988 The Iona Community

SANCTUS & BENEDICTUS

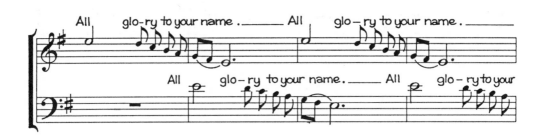

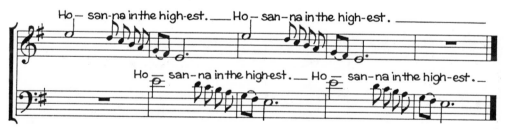

AGNUS DEI

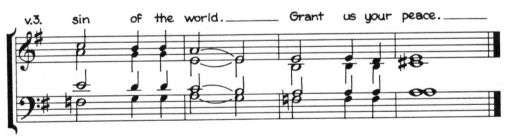

Music © 1988 The Iona Community

ENEMY OF APATHY
WILD GOOSE SONGS – VOLUME 2
Alphabetical Index of First Lines and Tunes
(Title, where different, is in italics)

ACKNOWLEDGEMENT

Thanks for permission to use the tune *Ho Ri Ho Ro*, by Alexander Sinclair, are due to the Sir Hugh Roberton Trust and Roberton Publications.

COPYRIGHT

OTHER PUBLICATIONS

The Iona Community has an increasing range of worship and resource materials, tapes etc., which may be purchased on a retail basis or wholesale. For a catalogue and further details, apply to Wild Goose Resources Group at the above address.

Wild Goose Publications
CURRENT PUBLICATIONS OF THE IONA COMMUNITY

THE WHOLE EARTH SHALL CRY GLORY   Paperback   ISBN 0 947988 00 9

THE WHOLE EARTH SHALL CRY GLORY   Hardback   ISBN 0 947988 04 1
Iona prayers by Rev. George F. MacLeod

THE IONA COMMUNITY WORSHIP BOOK   ISBN 0 947988 28 9
Iona Community

RE-INVENTING THEOLOGY   ISBN 0 947988 29 7
Ian M. Fraser

MEANING THE LORD'S PRAYER   ISBN 0 947988 30 0
George T. H. Reid

PARABLES AND PATTER   ISBN 0 947988 33 5
Erik Cramb

ROGER – An Extraordinary Peace Campaigner   ISBN 0 947988 38 6
Helen Steven

LIVING A COUNTERSIGN – From Iona To Basic Christian Communities   ISBN 0 947988 39 4
Ian Fraser

HEAVEN SHALL NOT WAIT (Wild Goose Songs Volume 1)   ISBN 0 947988 23 8
John Bell & Graham Maule

ENEMY OF APATHY (Wild Goose Songs Volume 2)   ISBN 0 947988 27 0
John Bell & Graham Maule

LOVE FROM BELOW (Wild Goose Songs Volume 3)   ISBN 0 947988 34 3
John Bell & Graham Maule

LOVE FROM BELOW – Cassette   No. IC/WGP/008
Wild Goose Worship Group

MANY AND GREAT (World Church Songs Volume 1)   ISBN 0 947988 40 8
John Bell & Graham Maule

MANY AND GREAT – Cassette   No. IC/WGP/009
Wild Goose Worship Group

SENT BY THE LORD (World Church Songs Volume 2)   ISBN 0 947988 44 0
John Bell & Graham Maule

SENT BY THE LORD – Cassette   No. IC/WGP/010
Wild Goose Worship Group

A TOUCHING PLACE – Cassette   No. IC/WGP/004
Wild Goose Worship Group

CLOTH FOR THE CRADLE – Cassette   No. IC/WGP/007
Wild Goose Worship Group

FOLLY AND LOVE – Cassette   No. IC/WGP/005
Iona Abbey

FREEDOM IS COMING – Cassette   No. IC/WGP/006

FREEDOM IS COMING   ISBN 0 947988 49 1
Utryck

PRAISING A MYSTERY   ISBN 0 947988 36 X
Brian Wren

BRING MANY NAMES   ISBN 0 947988 37 8
Brian Wren

WILD GOOSE PRINTS No. 1   ISBN 0 947988 06 8
John Bell & Graham Maule

WILD GOOSE PRINTS No. 2   ISBN 0 947988 10 6
John Bell & Graham Maule

WILD GOOSE PRINTS No. 3   ISBN 0 947988 24 6
John Bell & Graham Maule

WILD GOOSE PRINTS No. 4   ISBN 0 947988 35 1
John Bell & Graham Maule

WILD GOOSE PRINTS No. 5   ISBN 0 947988 41 6
John Bell & Graham Maule

WILD GOOSE PRINTS No. 6   ISBN 0 947988 42 4
John Bell & Graham Maule

EH . . . JESUS . . . YES, PETER . . .? Book 1   ISBN 0 947988 20 3
John Bell & Graham Maule

EH . . . JESUS . . . YES, PETER . . .? Book 2   ISBN 0 947988 31 9
John Bell & Graham Maule

EH . . . JESUS . . . YES, PETER . . .? Book 3   ISBN 0 947988 43 2
John Bell & Graham Maule